MIGHTY MILITARY MACHINES

Fighter Planes

Fearless Fliers

Karen and Glen Bledsoe

Enslow Publishers, Inc.
40 Industrial Road
Box 398
Berkeley Heights, NJ 07922
USA

http://www.enslow.com

Library of Congress Cataloging-in-Publication Data

Bledsoe, Karen E.
  Fighter planes : fearless fliers / by Karen and Glen Bledsoe.
      p. cm. — (Mighty military machines)
  Includes bibliographical references and index.
  ISBN-10: 0-7660-2660-4
  1. Eagle (Jet fighter plane)—Juvenile literature. 2. F-16 (Jet fighter plane)—Juvenile literature. 3. Hornet (Jet fighter plane)—Juvenile literature. 4. Fighter pilots—Training of—United States—Juvenile literature. I. Bledsoe, Glen. II. Title. III. Series.

    UG1242.F5B548 2006
    623.7'464—dc22

                                    2005037383
  ISBN-13: 978-0-7660-2660-5

Printed in the United States of America

10 9 8 7 6 5 4 3 2

To Our Readers:
We have done our best to make sure all Internet Addresses in this book were active and appropriate when we went to press. However, the author and the publisher have no control over and assume no liability for the material available on those Internet sites or on other Web sites they may link to. Any comments or suggestions can be sent by e-mail to comments@enslow.com or to the address on the back cover.

Contents

Chapter ONE

Surprise Mission

Gary Kurdys woke from a deep sleep to the ringing of his cell phone. He had finished a long night flying deliveries for Federal Express, his full-time job. The last thing he wanted was a phone call, cutting his sleep short. But Kurdys was also a Lieutenant Colonel for the Texas Air National Guard, and had to be ready for a call at any time.

Kurdys picked up the phone and heard the voice of his flight lead, the pilot in charge when they flew on military missions. "I'm sitting on alert. We're on battle stations ready alert."

Kurdys asked what it was all about.

"Have you seen the news?" his flight lead asked.

The date was September 11, 2001. When Kurdys switched on the television, he watched in disbelief as the second of two airliners crashed into the World Trade Center in New York City. Another plane had crashed into the Pentagon in Washington, D.C. A fourth went down in a field in Pennsylvania. Terrorists had used the four planes as weapons to attack American targets, and no one knew whether there would be more attacks.

Minutes later, Kurdys arrived at Ellington Field in Houston, Texas, and jumped into his F-16 fighter jet, where his crew chief strapped him in. The giant engines roared to life and Kurdys took off, flying as wingman alongside the flight lead's jet. Both jets raced along at 1,500 miles per hour (mph). Their target was in the air over the panhandle of Florida. But the location was all Kurdys knew. When he asked the flight lead for more information, the answer was, "You'll know what to do when you get there."

Kurdys could only imagine what the mission might be. Was there another plane still in the air? Would they have to intercept it and possibly attack it?

Less than an hour later, as they neared Florida, Kurdys spotted the target: a familiar blue 747. It was Air Force One, the president's plane. In response to the morning's attacks, Air Force One was flying President George W. Bush to safety. It was the job of the F-16 pilots to fly alongside Air Force One, ready to fight any opposing aircraft or missiles they might meet.

As Kurdys flew, he watched for unidentified aircraft and other dangers. Fortunately, they met no attackers. Kurdys helped take Air Force One to the nearest Air Force base, in Louisiana. Next, Kurdys and his partner escorted Air Force One and the president to another base, this time in Nebraska. There the president stayed until he could safely return to the White House.

FACTFILE

So You Want to Be a Fighter Jet Pilot?

Fighter pilots have one bit of advice for young people who want to someday be pilots: start now!

Those who want to get into pilot training programs work hard to earn high grades in school. The written test to get into the program is tough. It includes math, science, writing, and knowledge of flight and airplanes. Once in the program, candidates must study or work on flight training nearly every waking hour.

Candidates must be physically fit, because flying a jet is physically grueling. Candidates must pass a fitness test to enter the program, and stay fit during their career. Most military pilots participated in school or community sports, or stuck to a good personal fitness program, so they were already well prepared.

▲ President George W. Bush (on the bottom step) exits Air Force One in Washington, D.C., on September 11, 2001.

What Is a Fighter Jet?

The F-16 that Kurdys flew on his mission was a modern fighter jet. A fighter jet is a small, fast jet-propelled plane loaded with high-powered weapons. It may carry one or two people. Before the 1960s, fighter jets were designed to attack other airplanes. But today's fighter jets often have many roles.

Besides fighting other aircraft, they may attack targets on the ground using laser-controlled missiles and rockets. Some fighter jets carry missiles to destroy opposing missiles that target other fighter jets. They may escort other planes, such as large cargo planes that carry goods and supplies, planes that transport troops, or special planes carrying national leaders or other important people.

Fighter jets are powered by jet engines. A jet engine pulls air in through the front and forces it out the back of the engine. This drives the aircraft forward through the air much faster than a propeller. While propeller-driven planes can reach top speeds of about 500 mph, fighter jets can reach almost four times that speed.

Modern fighter jets are equipped with powerful weapons, including machine guns and missiles. Hi-tech computer systems and onboard radar systems, which use radio waves to locate objects such as other planes, help pilots navigate day and night and in all types of weather. Though the pilot is secured in the seat, everything needed to fly the plane is within reach, from hand controls to head-up displays projected on the visor of the

◀ Air Force crew chiefs move a jet engine into position to be installed in an F-16 fighter jet.

pilot's helmet. As U.S. Navy Lieutenant Dan Hughes says of flying his F-18 Hornet fighter jet, "You don't fly the jet, you strap it on."

FACTFILE

The Crew Chief

Air Force Staff Sergeant Matthew Perry is used to working in all conditions: the blazing heat of summer, freezing winter cold, and sudden red alerts, when everyone runs for cover from enemy attacks. Perry is a crew chief stationed at a U.S. Air Force base in Iraq. It is his job to make sure that the F-16 fighter jet he is assigned to stays in perfect working order.

"As a crew chief, you have to enjoy working in the cold, in the heat, and in the rain. You have to enjoy getting your hands dirty," says Perry.

As soon as his assigned fighter jet lands from a mission, Perry and his assistant go to work. The entire jet must be inspected for damage and problems, which must be fixed before its next mission. They have to work fast, because the jet may need to take off again in a few hours. The crew chief makes sure the jet has fuel and that all systems work perfectly before the jet takes off. Finally, the chief helps buckle the pilot into the cockpit.

"Seeing your jet take off two or three times a day and return home safely each time—that's the real reward," says Perry. "Having that pilot climb out and say, 'Great job, chief' makes it worth it."

Chapter TWO

Fighter Planes to Fighter Jets

The modern fighter jet is not just a vehicle. The whole plane is the pilot's weapon in a battle against enemy forces. But hi-tech fighter jets are not the only planes that have been used in war. The history of fighter planes goes back to the invention of the airplane itself.

Early Fighter Planes

After many experiments with designing and flying gliders, Orville and Wilbur Wright made the first successful flight of an engine-powered airplane, the Wright Flyer, in 1903. Within a few years the Wrights were supplying planes for the very first Army Air Service, which later became the U.S. Air Force.

Another inventor, Glenn Curtiss, created floats that allowed planes to land on water. He invented a ramp for planes to take off from the deck of a large ship, creating the first aircraft carrier. Soon Curtiss was supplying the U.S. Navy with aircraft. When World War I broke out in Europe in 1914, the world saw the first use of airplanes in battle.

These first military planes were simple machines compared with today's aircraft. They were just wooden frames covered with tough canvas fabric. The planes were powered by gasoline engines that turned propellers. The pilot sat in an open cockpit. Pilots carried pistols to shoot at

The pilot sat in an open cockpit and carried a pistol to shoot at opposing pilots.

opposing pilots. The pilot or a second crewman called an observer might carry small bombs to drop by hand on targets below.

The first weapon designed for airplanes was a machine gun that fired forward through the propeller blades. The shots had to be carefully timed to pass between the blades without hitting them. Some pilots crashed when the timing was off and the machine gun splintered their propellers. However, a forward-firing machine gun was a useful weapon. A pilot could fire at an opposing plane as he chased it, rather than pull alongside an enemy plane and shoot at the pilot with a pistol. With the invention of forward-firing guns, military airplanes became true fighter planes.

By World War II (1939–1945), fighter planes became larger and more powerful fighting machines. They were built with metal frames covered with sheet metal. The cockpit was enclosed in glass to protect the pilot from high winds. Larger and more powerful engines helped planes fly faster in order to outfly bombers and other fighters. Fighter planes became the tigers of the sky, shooting down enemy bombers, or fighting one another in spectacular "dogfights" in the air.

Engineers were always designing faster planes. By the end of World War II, a new plane made its first appearance in battle: the fighter jet.

The First Fighter Jets

In 1944, American and British military pilots were surprised by a fast plane with swept-back wings that rocketed past them. It was the Me-262, built by the German company Messerschmitt and powered by a pair of jet engines. It was faster than any other plane at the time. The new jet could chase down fighter planes and attack bombers.

The United States, Britain, and their allies were fighting against the Axis nations of Germany, Italy,

The P-80 Shooting Star was the first American fighter jet. ▲
It was developed in the 1940s and used in combat during the
Korean War (1950–1953).

and Japan. If Germany had a new jet superweapon, that meant trouble for the Allies.

The United States and Britain worked hard to design jet aircraft of their own. The U.S. Army Air Forces (as the former Army Air Service was renamed in 1941) completed work on the P-80 Shooting Star in 1945, but a P-80 crashed when one of its engines caught fire, killing the test pilot and delaying further tests. The British had better success with the Gloster Meteor, which entered the war in mid-1944.

After the war, the United States developed new jet-powered fighter planes. Fighter jets were used in the Korean War in the early 1950s, and in the Vietnam War in the 1960s and 1970s. Today, all military fighter planes are fighter jets.

Features of a Fighter Jet

What distinguishes a fighter jet from earlier types of fighter planes is its jet engines. Jet engines made the Messerschmitt Me-262 fly faster than propeller-driven fighter planes. Top speed for the Me-262 was 540 mph. By comparison, the P-47 Thunderbolt, one of the fastest U.S. fighter planes during World War II, flew at 467 mph. Jet-propelled aircraft today can fly even faster, speeding along at over 1,900 mph.

▼ The P-47 Thunderbolt was one of America's fastest fighter planes in World War II. A pair of P-47s were the first to shoot down a German Me-262 fighter jet.

FACTFILE

Automatic Flying

It takes a tremendous amount of concentration to fly a fighter jet at super speeds while dodging missiles and other dangers or searching for other aircraft. Fortunately, fighter pilots have onboard computer systems to help them. One system is the autopilot system.

The autopilot system includes a computer that reads the plane's position using the plane's altimeter, an instrument that measures how high a plane is above sea level. The computer also uses information from satellites that assists with navigation. After the pilot enters the location of the target or destination into the computer, the computer sends electrical signals to the throttle, which controls the engine and changes airspeed. It also sends signals to the rudder to help turn the plane. This keeps the plane on course until it reaches its destination, or the pilot changes the information. It moves fuel from one tank to another to help balance a plane in the air as well.

Autopilots are a big help during routine flying, doing up to 80 percent of the pilot's work. However, no computer system has been built that can cope with the rapidly changing dangers of flying into battle. That is where human pilots still rely on their own training, wits, and intelligence.

Modern fighters use avionics systems to help the pilot fly. Avionics systems are electrical systems on board an airplane that control communication (how pilots talk to each other and their commanders

▲ U.S. Air Force F-16 pilot "Split" looks out from his head-up display after a mission in Iraq.

FACTFILE

A New Head-up System

Pilots who are chasing other aircraft have to turn their planes to point their weapons. But a new invention may change that. At a U.S. Air Force base located in Germany, American F-16 fighter pilots are testing a new helmet targeting system.

The system is an advanced head-up display that shows flight information on the helmet's visor. But it has one added feature: with only a turn of the head, the pilot can aim a missile instead of turning the whole plane to aim. All the pilot has to do is look at the target to lock on the weapons and fire. At $100,000 each, the new systems are expensive, but they make flying safer. Pilots can keep their attention focused outside the cockpit instead of looking down at the weapons controls.

on the ground), navigation (how pilots direct their planes), and weapons. An autopilot system helps keep the plane flying, while a flight management system keeps the plane on course.

Fighter jets often use head-up displays. These displays may be placed in front of the windscreen, or front window, of a jet. Newer systems are placed on the pilot's visor. Computer systems project information from the plane's instruments on the display, such as navigation information. Head-up displays help prevent midair accidents because pilots do not have to look down at their instruments while they are flying or aiming weapons.

Chapter THREE

F-15 Eagle

Air Force Captain Mary Melfi, a Weapons Systems Officer, and her pilot, Major Bob Saleska, took off in a two-seater F-15 Strike Eagle over Iraq on March 30, 2003. Their mission: to protect a U-2 surveillance aircraft, or spy plane. U-2s have no weapons, and often need fighter jets to protect them.

"We were pretty ho-hum going out the door," Saleska said. Other such missions had gone off without a hitch. They did not expect to do more than fly all day in an assigned pattern on this one, refueling their plane in midair from a tanker as needed. It looked like this would be another routine mission.

But several hours into the mission, the U-2 spotted a Scud missile launcher. The Iraqi army used Scud missiles (large, rocket-powered weapons) against other nations. Suddenly, Saleska and Melfi's mission changed: now they were instructed to destroy the launcher. As Saleska flew toward the target, Melfi checked the weapons systems.

As they neared the launcher, they flew into a storm of anti-aircraft fire. Bright trails from missiles shot up around them. Saleska "jinked," maneuvering the plane rapidly, to avoid getting hit. Melfi searched for the target amid the fire. Finally she could see it, but now they were too low on fuel to complete the mission. Saleska turned the plane and darted away.

He headed to the tanker plane to fill up the F-15, then flew back over the Scud site and back into the anti-aircraft fire.

Captain Melfi hit the "fire" button, sending a guided bomb straight at the target.

"At that point we decided to turn inbound and [start] the target attack," Melfi added. She pointed a laser beam on the Scud launcher. She hit the "fire" button, sending a guided bomb straight at the target. It exploded, but at that moment another gunner on the ground opened fire at them. Saleska dodged away. Had Melfi hit the target?

Saleska took the plane back in moments later to find out if Melfi had scored a hit. She had, and Saleska took them out of the area once and for all.

By the time they finished their not-so-routine mission, Saleska and Melfi had been in the air for nine straight hours. Through teamwork, they had destroyed an Iraqi Scud missile launcher.

The F-15 Eagle

Melfi and Saleska flew their mission in an F-15E Strike Eagle, the two-seater version of the F-15 Eagle. Both are dual-engine fighter jets. They can fly up to 3,450 miles without refueling. That is farther than the distance across the United States! The original F-15s were designed in the 1960s and built in the 1970s. They have been updated through the years as new technology becomes available.

The F-15 is highly maneuverable, meaning it turns quickly without losing speed. Its low weight compared with its large wing size helps make it maneuverable. The comparison of weight and wing size is called wing loading.

Fighter Jet of the Future

Engineers are always working on new designs to make fighter jets faster, more powerful, and easier to fly, with more advanced weapons and better computer controls. Sometimes engineers create updated versions of existing planes. The F-15 is an example of a plane that has been updated with the latest technology.

However, the U.S. Air Force says that newer aircraft made in Russia, France, and Germany are better than the most up-to-date F-15s. The newer planes are faster and more maneuverable. They also have more advanced firepower, radar, and other systems.

In order to compete, engineers have come up with an entirely new design. The plane that the engineers designed is the F/A-22 Raptor. It has new long-range sensors that allow it to detect aircraft before it is detected. Its extremely powerful engines allow the Raptor to cruise at top speed longer than other fighter jets can. It is lightweight and has a wing design that may make it the most maneuverable fighter jet in the air.

At $256.9 million, the Raptor is much more expensive than the $27.9 million F-15, and has not been tested in combat. It has not yet been adopted by the U.S. military, but it could be the fighter jet of the future.

Flying at two and a half times the speed of sound, a pilot does not have the chance to look down at the control panels. The F-15 Eagle uses a head-up display projected on a panel on the windscreen to provide the information the pilot needs. It can be seen in all kinds of weather and in daylight and darkness.

▼ A U.S. Air Force ground crew prepares to load a self-guided bomb onto an F-15.

FACTFILE

The F-15 Eagle
Used as a fighter and strike-attack aircraft
Length: 63.8 feet
Height: 18.5 feet
Wingspan: 42.8 feet
Maximum takeoff weight:
    68,000 pounds
Top speed: Mach 2.5 (over 1,900 mph)
Weapons: cannons, missiles, laser-guided bombs,
    and machine guns
Cost: $27.9 million

F-15s carry pulse-Doppler radar, electronic systems that help pilots find both high-flying and low-flying targets far beyond the range that the pilot can see. The advanced radar system plays a big role in the jet's defense. It can spot fast-moving targets above and below the jet, and send information directly to the weapons systems to lock onto the targets. It can also quickly spot opposing aircraft during dogfights and display information about them on the pilot's head-up display. A central computer identifies whether nearby aircraft are "friend or foe." The computer can also send signals to friendly, or allied, ground stations so they will not attack the jet by mistake.

The F-15 carries a wide range of high-powered weapons, including missiles, laser-guided bombs, and machine guns.

Chapter FOUR

F-16 Fighting Falcon

On May 11, 2005, the alarm went off at Andrews Air Force Base in Maryland. Lieutenant Colonel Tim Lehmann and his wingman from the Air National Guard's 121st Fighter Squadron took off minutes later in their F-16 fighter jets.

An unidentified aircraft was heading toward Washington, D.C. No one knew if this aircraft was piloted by someone who had simply gotten lost, or if it was piloted by a terrorist who planned to crash the plane into a building. As a result of the terrorist attacks of September 11, 2001, aircraft are not allowed to fly over the nation's capital. Pilots who

A U.S. Air Force F-16 Fighting Falcon flies through the air during a combat mission in Iraq in 2004. One of the missiles it carries can be seen under the wing, next to the large jet engine.

fly into restricted zones are warned. If they do not stop, military aircraft are sent to intercept them, and, if necessary, shoot them down. Lehmann hoped to simply intercept the aircraft. But he was ready to shoot it down if it looked like it was threatening the city.

Twelve miles north of the capital, Lehmann and his partner spotted the aircraft. It was a private Cessna, a small, propeller-driven airplane. Two Customs Agency planes were already following it, but they moved away as the F-16 fighters took over.

If the plane flew closer to the U.S. capital, the F-16 pilots might be ordered to shoot it down.

Following the Cessna was difficult. It flew much slower than the jets could fly. They could not pull alongside to signal the pilot. Lehmann and his partner flew a wide oval pattern around the plane. First Lehmann dropped a flare to get the pilot's attention, but there was no response. Then his partner dropped a flare.

The Cessna pilot still did not respond. The situation was looking more and more like a possible terrorist attack. If the plane flew closer to the U.S. capital, the F-16 pilots might be ordered to shoot it down. In the meantime, many buildings in Washington, D.C., were evacuated and people poured into the streets.

Finally, after Lehmann dropped another flare, he heard the pilot's nervous voice on the radio. This was not a terrorist, but a lost pilot who now realized with horror that he had accidentally flown off course and had been the target of fighter jets. The pilot obeyed the command to fly to Frederick Municipal Airport in Maryland. Once on the ground, he was arrested. The tense situation came to a quiet end in just over fifteen minutes. Everyone was relieved that this was not terrorist attack and that the aircraft did not have to be shot down. But it was a close call.

▼ In 2005 the pilot of this small aircraft mistakenly flew into restricted airspace over Washington, D.C. Two F-16 fighter jets were called in to intercept the plane in case it was part of a terrorist attack.

FACTFILE

The F-16 Fighting Falcon

Used as a multi-role fighter
Length: 49 feet, 5 inches
Height: 16 feet
Wingspan: 32 feet, 8 inches
Maximum takeoff weight: 37,500 pounds
Top speed: Mach 2 (1,500 mph)
Weapons: M-61A1 cannon, air-to-air missiles,
    air-to-surface missiles
Cost: $14.6 million

The F-16

The F-16 Fighting Falcon is sometimes called the "Viper," which was its code name during early development. Used mainly by the Air Force, this single-engine fighter is a favorite among pilots and ground crews because it is reliable and easy to take care of. The F-16 flew for the first time in 1976. Since then, several models have been developed. The Fighting Falcon is the latest.

The Fighting Falcon is small and highly maneuverable. It is a multi-role fighter, which means it can do more than one job. For example, it is fitted with a built-in M61 Vulcan cannon which launches air-to-air missiles for attacking other fighter planes. It can also carry missiles or bombs for attacking ground targets.

One unusual feature of the F-16 is its control stick. While most fighter jets have a control stick mounted in the center, between the pilot's knees, the F-16 has a side-mounted control stick. It is designed to give fine control during high-speed turns, such as a pilot might have to make during a dogfight. In early designs, the stick did not move at all, and the plane responded to the pressure of the pilot's hand. But pilots found that this was too tiring to use, so engineers designed the stick to move slightly.

The F-16's bubble canopy is also designed for air-to-air dogfights. The bubble canopy, which is like a curved window that covers the cockpit, gives the pilot a view of the sky almost entirely around the aircraft.

▼ The bubble canopy of an F-16 allows the pilot to see in all directions. These two Air Force F-16s are flying over Florida.

FACTFILE

Call Names

Fighter jet pilots often go by special call names. Call names are short and easy to pronounce. This makes it easy for ground controllers to identify pilots on the radio. The military also requires pilots to use their call names instead of their real names when talking on the radio or to reporters. This is a safety measure to protect pilots' identities from enemies.

But pilots do not always get cool call names such as "Maverick" or "Duke." In fact, pilots do not choose their call names at all. Instead, junior officers draw up a list of possible names, and a senior officer chooses one for each pilot. Some names may be funny or even unflattering, but each one is short and easy to remember. Some names used by pilots in the Navy and the Air Force include Duff, Mumbles, Scorch, Lamb, Urchin, and Smash.

The Fighting Falcon can fly more than five hundred miles, attack its target, and return home. This is further than most opposing aircraft. If necessary, it can fly higher than fifty thousand feet. It is designed for all kinds of weather. Opposing aircraft may fly low to avoid radar detection, but the F-16 has advanced radar to find low-flying aircraft.

The F-16 fighter flew in the Persian Gulf War of 1991. F-16s were involved in both air combat and air strikes on ground forces. Today, F-16 fighters still fly in the Persian Gulf to support American troops in Iraq.

Chapter FIVE

F/A-18 Hornet

On September 11, 2001, when terrorists attacked the United States, the aircraft carrier U.S.S. *Enterprise* had just finished a six-month cruise. Navy Lieutenant and pilot Dan Hughes was looking forward to going home. But when he saw the news that day, he had a feeling that the homecoming would be a bit late.

Hughes was right. The *Enterprise* was the closest aircraft carrier to Afghanistan, where terrorists were believed to have been trained. When rulers in Afghanistan would not help the United States find the training camps, the United States struck back. The *Enterprise* would need to stay in the area.

The United States would need to use the fighter jets on the carrier in its attacks on Afghanistan.

Hughes flew his F/A-18 Hornet in bombing raids over Afghanistan throughout October 2001. On one mission, his target was a place in northern Afghanistan used by the terrorist group al-Qaeda, headed by Osama bin Laden.

The trip took six hours total, from takeoff to landing. The Hornet did not carry enough fuel for the entire trip, so Hughes had to refuel in midair. He met up with a tanker plane over Pakistan. He skillfully held his fighter in position for the fifteen minutes required to fill the Hornet's tanks.

The jet jerked in the air as the two-thousand-pound bomb dropped toward the ground.

Hughes continued on until he reached his target. He swooped down and dropped a "smart bomb," or self-guided weapon. The jet jerked in the air as the two-thousand-pound bomb dropped toward the ground. The smart bomb carried a computer chip programmed with the target's position. Signals from satellites in space guided the bomb toward the target. The bomb hit and the target was destroyed.

Hughes zoomed away, but soon anti-aircraft fire exploded around him. He maneuvered his jet to avoid it. Night was falling as Hughes rose into

▲ An Air Force KC-10 tanker jet refuels an F/A-18 Hornet in the skies of the Middle East.

the darkening sky and flew beyond the reach of the weapons. Once out of Afghanistan, he refueled again in midair, then headed back to the *Enterprise*, waiting in the Persian Gulf.

Hughes had to land on the deck of the aircraft carrier, a small moving target in the dark. Though he slowed his plane down as much as he could to land, the F/A-18 was screaming along at 150 mph when it hit the deck. A special hook attached to its tail, the tailhook, caught one of the cables on the deck designed to catch jets as they land. The jet jerked to a stop in just under three seconds.

A six-hour flight, two tricky midair refuelings, a guided bomb, enemy fire, and a tough landing in the dark—all in a day's work for an F/A-18 combat pilot.

The F/A-18 Hornet

The F/A-18 Hornet and the larger F/A-18 Super Hornet are twin-engine all-weather fighter and attack planes. (The "F/A" in their names stands for "fighter" and "attack.") These single-seat jets, flown by the U.S. Navy and used as strike fighters (planes that attack ground targets), are often the first planes in the air when there is a conflict. Two-seat Hornets and Super Hornets, flown by the Marines, are used as fighters and for attack and reconnaissance, or information-gathering, missions.

The first Hornet models were tested in 1978, but the F/A-18 Hornet was not used until 1983. The Super Hornet was ready for military use in 1997. The Hornet saw its first military action in Operation

FACTFILE

Goodwill Ambassadors

Fighter jets are used by the military, mostly for battle. The planes are designed as weapons, and have no civilian, or nonmilitary, uses.

However, there is one place where fighter jets are used outside of battle: flight demonstration squadrons. The Navy's Blue Angels and the Air Force's Thunderbirds perform at air shows to provide exciting entertainment, and to get people interested in the military. In 1992, the Blue Angels flew their first European tour in nineteen years. Among the countries they visited were Russia, Romania, and Bulgaria. For many years, these countries had been rivals of the United States. The pilots said it felt strange to fly alongside Russian military jets. But they were glad to make friends of old enemies and to swap tales with Russian pilots.

A cloud of water vapor builds up around a Navy F/A-18 ▲ Super Hornet as it flies at nearly 800 mph. The vapor cloud is common at certain altitudes, speeds, and air temperatures.

Desert Storm in 1991, when it showed how useful it was by shooting down opposing aircraft and bombing ground targets during the same mission. Before the Hornet, it would have taken two separate aircraft to complete these missions.

The Hornet was one of the first aircraft to use multi-function displays. At the push of a button, the pilot can view information needed for fighter mode (for air-to-air fights), which includes the ability to look up or down and track other aircraft. The display also shows information for attack mode (for attacking ground targets), which includes a map of the area below the aircraft and locations of targets.

It was also designed to be easy to care for and to survive attacks with little damage. Hornets hit by

Dangerous Landings

Landing a fighter jet on the deck of an aircraft carrier is difficult and dangerous. Pilots describe the landing procedure as a "controlled crash."

The fighter jets come roaring down at high speeds, often over 150 mph. To make sure that all jets stop before reaching the end of the runway on a carrier, the jets are fitted with tailhooks. A tailhook is a sturdy hook at the tail of the aircraft that hooks onto strong cables strung across the ship's flight deck. The cables, called arresting gear, jerk

the plane to a halt in just three seconds.

Not only do pilots have to hit a very narrow target, but they also must be at just the right height. If the jet is too high, the tailhook will not catch the arresting gear and the pilot has to quickly make an emergency takeoff to avoid crashing into the sea. If too low, the plane will smack into the ship.

Pilots practice takeoffs and landings day and night to prevent accidents. Aircraft carriers may carry eighty or more aircraft, so planes are always taking off and landing. This makes the flight deck of an aircraft carrier a busy, noisy place!

surface-to-air missiles during Operation Desert Storm made it home, were repaired, and were back in the air the next day with far less downtime than other fighter planes. The Hornet's parts are made to be installed on and taken off the jet easily. Entire sections of the aircraft can be lifted out and replaced quickly.

The Hornet and Super Hornet are extremely maneuverable planes. They can change course quickly in the air to avoid enemy fire. The plane uses a fly-by-wire system that allows rudders, flaps, and other parts that control the plane's flight to be moved electronically. The Super Hornet is used by the Blue Angels, the Navy's Flight Demonstration Squadron. In the Blue Angels' demonstrations, the jet is pushed to the extreme as the pilots carry out their high-speed stunts. The Hornet's maneuverability makes it ideal for these dramatic, thrilling stunts.

FACT FILE

The F/A-18 Hornet

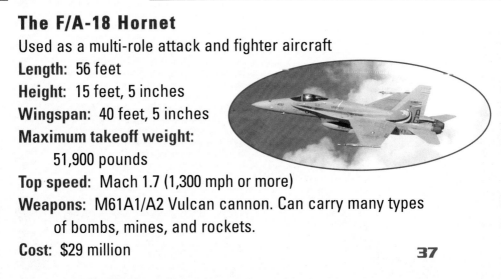

Used as a multi-role attack and fighter aircraft

Length: 56 feet

Height: 15 feet, 5 inches

Wingspan: 40 feet, 5 inches

Maximum takeoff weight:
    51,900 pounds

Top speed: Mach 1.7 (1,300 mph or more)

Weapons: M61A1/A2 Vulcan cannon. Can carry many types
    of bombs, mines, and rockets.

Cost: $29 million

Chapter SIX

Training to Be a Fighter Pilot

When young men and women first join the air defense branches of the military, they may dream of being fighter pilots. Certainly fighter pilots get the glory in the news, in movies, and in video games. But becoming a fighter pilot is a long and difficult road. It takes training, determination, discipline, and a lot of hard work.

Learning to Fly

Student pilots are selected from military officers, officers in training, Reserve Officer Training Corps (ROTC) at colleges and universities, Officer Training

School, and military academies. All fighter pilots must begin with Introductory Flight Training (IFT). This training is taught by civilian flight instructors. Students start by flying small, propeller-driven airplanes like the Cessna 152. This training takes fifty hours, and students earn their private pilot certificate when they finish.

JSUPT

After earning their basic pilot certificate, students from the Air Force and Navy enter Joint Specialized Undergraduate Pilot Training (JSUPT). In JSUPT student pilots train for different kinds of military flight missions. To get into JSUPT candidates must have letters of recommendation from their superior officers, as well as pass two written tests. One of these, the Armed Forces Officer Qualifying Test (AFOQT), is a long and difficult test that takes five hours to finish. Candidates have

Becoming a fighter pilot takes training, determination, discipline, and a lot of hard work.

to be good at math, science, written English, and must know a lot about airplanes and flying to pass the test.

When the written tests are over, JSUPT candidates have a different test to pass. This is the Fighter Aircrew Conditioning Test (FACT). In this tough fitness test, candidates are challenged in areas related to flying a plane, such as aerobic fitness and muscle strength. Candidates must be in excellent physical condition to pass.

Once in the program, JSUPT students move through three demanding training phases. In Phase 1, students spend twelve hours a day learning about military flight and aircraft. They also have to learn things such as how to parachute safely to the ground.

▼ Two Air Force pilot candidates study the controls of a computerized training device during the first part of their training.

FACTFILE

Could You Pass the FACT?

The Fighter Aircrew Conditioning Test (FACT) is the physical fitness test that all pilot candidates must pass early in their training. Throughout their careers, pilots must maintain at least this level of fitness and are retested from time to time. The test is made up of eight exercises. (Do not start a fitness program or try these exercises without the supervision of a gym teacher, coach, or trainer. Without proper training, you could be seriously injured.)

To test strength, students have to lift a certain amount of weight with their arms or legs ten to fifteen times. The amount of weight depends on their body weight. For the bench press, students lie on their backs and lift weights with their arms as heavy as 80 percent of their body weight. That means a one hundred-pound person would have to lift eighty pounds.

To test endurance, or how long a person can be active without tiring, candidates have to do push-ups, crunches, and leg presses at least twenty times in a row. Fifty times in a row is the target.

If you think you could pass the FACT now, great! But keep on working out—with a coach, of course—because the bigger a person gets, the harder the test gets!

In Phase 2, students get their first training as jet pilots. With the help of a teacher who flies as co-pilot, students learn how to take off and land safely. Then they learn to fly loops and rolls. Once they are ready, students learn how to fly on instruments alone,

which prepares them to fly at night, in fog, and at other times when there is poor visibility. Instruments tell pilots where they are, and help locate opposing aircraft and targets.

In Phase 3 of JSUPT, students move into a training track that determines what kind of pilot they will become. Sometimes students have a choice. Sometimes they are placed in a track

Pilot candidates get ready to fly their training jets at an ▲ Air Force base in Oklahoma. In Phase 2 of JSUPT, trainees get to fly jets for the first time.

according to their skills or according to what jobs the military needs to fill. Tracks include training to be transport pilots, who fly planes that carry cargo and troops; helicopter pilots; tanker pilots, who fly

▲ Being a fighter pilot may seem more exciting, but some military pilots choose to fly transport planes like this one because they can log much more flying time. These pilots have just completed a mission bringing supplies to areas devastated by a tsunami in 2004.

planes that carry fuel for the midair refueling of other planes; or pilots of fighter jets and bombers. The length of training in Phase 3 depends on the track the student enters. It can be anywhere from 24 to 28 weeks, with 105 to 120 hours of flying time.

From start to finish, JSUPT training takes about one year. Graduates receive their silver wings and become pilots. After graduation, pilots who did the best in JSUPT often get their first choice in assignments, and often their first choice is to be a fighter pilot.

Life After the Military

When pilots leave the military, they may continue flying as civilian pilots. Many go on to become passenger jet pilots for major airlines. Others may fly for the postal service or for delivery services such as UPS or FedEx, which transport mail and packages all over the world. Some become civilian trainers working for the military. They give pilot candidates their first flying lessons. Police and emergency medical services often need pilots with military experience because they are used to flying in bad conditions.

Some pilots plan ahead when they choose a career path in the military. If they think they may want to be airline pilots in the future, they often choose to fly transport and tanker planes in the military rather than fighters and bombers. Why? Pilots who fly transports and tankers usually spend more time in the air than fighter pilots. When it comes to finding a job as an airline pilot, flight experience counts.

Whether they fly fighter jets or other aircraft, military pilots train throughout their careers. Learning new skills keeps them the best in the skies.

anti-aircraft fire—Missiles and rockets fired from the ground at planes in the air.

avionics—Aircraft electronics. The electrical systems on an airplane that control communication and other things.

call name—A nickname that pilots use to identify themselves to other pilots without using their real names.

cockpit—The space inside an airplane where the pilot sits.

dogfight—A battle between two fighter planes in the air.

flight lead—The lead pilot on a mission with more than one fighter flying together.

head-up display—A display shown on the windscreen of a plane or on the visor of the pilot's helmet that allows the pilot to see both the plane's controls and where the plane is flying at the same time.

missile—A rocket-powered weapon that carries an explosive bomb.

navigation—Guiding aircraft or ships along a course.

propeller—A set of blades that turn in the air. The propeller forces air in one direction. This gives the force that moves an airplane forward.

radar—A tool that detects objects by sending out radio waves that bounce off of the objects.

reconnaissance—Exploring an area to gather military information.

surveillance—Watching or spying on people or groups over time to learn what they are doing.

wingman—A pilot that flies behind and to the side of the flight lead when several fighters are flying in formation.

Books

Graham, Ian. *Attack Fighters.* Chicago, Ill.: Heinemann Library, 2003.

Green, Michael, and Gladys Green. *Air Superiority Fighters: The F/A-22 Raptors.* Mankato, Minn.: Capstone Press, 2003.

Holden, Henry M. *Aircraft: Navy Combat Aircraft and Pilots.* Berkeley Heights, N.J.: Enslow Publishers, Inc., 2002.

Seidman, David. *The F/A-18 Hornet.* New York: Rosen Publishing Group, 2003.

Shaefer, A.R. and Raymond L. Puffer. *Jet Fighter Planes.* Mankato, Minn.: Edge Books/Capstone Press, 2004.

Stone, Lynn. *F-15 Eagle.* Vero Beach, Fla.: Rourke Publishing, 2004.

Stone, Lynn. *F-16 Fighting Falcon.* Vero Beach, Fla.: Rourke Publishing, 2004.

Internet Addresses

http://www.blueangels.navy.mil
   The Blue Angels

http://thunderbirds.airforce.com
   The Thunderbirds

http://www.af.mil/
   factsheets/factsheet.
   asp?id=199
   Detailed Information
   on the F-22A Raptor

INDEX